PRIMARY SOURCES OF THE THIRTEEN COLONIES AND THE LOST COLONY™

A Primary Source History of the Colony of
SOUTH CAROLINA

HEATHER HASAN

rosen central
Primary Source™

The Rosen Publishing Group, Inc., New York

*To my sister, Lee. You have taught me so much through the years.
How fortunate I am to have a big sister like you!*

Published in 2006 by The Rosen Publishing Group, Inc.
29 East 21st Street, New York, NY 10010

Library of Congress Cataloging-in-Publication Data

Hasan, Heather.
A primary source history of the colony of South Carolina/Heather Hasan.
    p. cm.—(Primary sources of the thirteen colonies and the Lost Colony)
Includes bibliographical references.
ISBN 1-4042-0436-9 (lib. bdg.)
ISBN 1-4042-0667-1 (pbk. bdg.)
1. South Carolina—History—Colonial period, ca. 1600–1775—Juvenile literature.
2. South Carolina—History—1775–1865—Juvenile literature.
I. Title. II. Series.

F269.3.H37 2005
975.7–dc22

2004020373

Manufactured in the United States of America

On the front cover: *Brevis Narratio* by Theodore de Bry and Jacques Lemoyne de Morgues. It is housed in the Service Historique de la Marine in Vincennes, France.

CONTENTS

INTRODUCTION

S outh Carolina is a very small state. It has a total area of only 31,000 square miles (79,487 square kilometers). In fact, it is the smallest state in the southeastern region of the United States.

This small state is wedged between North Carolina to the north and Georgia to the west and south. To the east, South Carolina is separated from the western coast of Africa by more than 3,000 miles (4,828 km) of Atlantic Ocean.

Despite its small size, South Carolina has abundant natural beauty and vegetation. The state is separated into three natural regions: the Blue Ridge, the Piedmont, and the Atlantic Coastal Plain.

An Early History

The Blue Ridge region is named after the Blue Ridge Mountains, which cover the northwestern part of the state. Here, there are dozens of beautiful waterfalls.

Next to Blue Ridge is the Piedmont. This area is a land of rolling hills and valleys.

The Atlantic Coastal Plain is flat and low and covers two-thirds of the state. This area includes sand hills, swamps, marshland, and beaches. It also includes a gently sloping region with warm, wet soil, which is perfect for farming.

For thousands of years before the first European settlers arrived in present-day South Carolina, the state was occupied by Native Americans. The first Native Americans arrived in South Carolina about 10,000 years ago. At first, these ancient people supported themselves by hunting and fishing, but about 3,000 years ago, they learned how to farm.

By the time the first Europeans entered what is now South Carolina 500 years ago, there were more than 20,000 Native

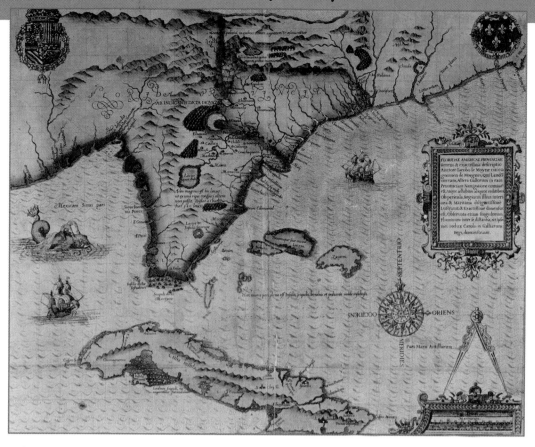

This map of the southeastern coast of what is now America was created in 1591 by Theodore de Bry as part of his "Americae" series. When de Bry created this map, there was a large Native American population in the area known today as South Carolina. However, Europeans knew little about the various Native American tribes. Europeans also knew little about American geography relative to what we know today. This is evident in this wildly inaccurate map. At the very bottom of the map is Cuba. Directly above Cuba is what is today's Florida.

Americans flourishing there. These people were separated into at least twenty-five distinct groups called tribes. Although Native Americans left no written record, historians have learned a lot about them from artifacts and oral traditions.

Of the more than twenty-five tribes living in South Carolina, the largest was the Cherokee. The Cherokees lived in the foothills of today's Blue Ridge Mountains in villages surrounded by log walls. The men hunted bear, deer, and other wild animals. They used the skins for clothing. The Cherokees also farmed. They grew corn, squash, beans, and melons.

The Catawba, another major tribe, lived in the northeastern part of the state, along the banks of the Catawba River. Fittingly, the name Catawba means "river people." The people of this tribe used bent saplings and tree bark to build their homes.

Another large tribe was the Yemassee. These people lived in the southern part of what is now South Carolina, near the mouth of the Savannah River, which separates the state from its southern neighbor, Georgia. The Yemassees spoke Muskogee, the language of the Creek tribe. They built their homes using grass, bark, and palmetto leaves.

These and other Native American groups, such as the Waccamaw, the Santee, and the Cusabo, were thriving when the first European settlers arrived in South Carolina. Today, only about 12,000 Native Americans live there. Sadly, when white settlers arrived, many Native Americans died from the diseases the settlers brought. Some Native Americans were enslaved, and others were later pushed from their land onto reservations. In the following chapters we'll learn of the European settlement and colonization of what we now know as South Carolina.

CHAPTER 1

In the early sixteenth century, Europe was in turmoil. The Protestant Reformation, which took place in the 1500s, began when a group of people (later called Protestants) voiced their belief that the Roman Catholic Church was corrupt. This led to religious wars between the Protestants and the Roman Catholics.

The Middle Ages (AD 500–1400) had also just ended in Europe at that time. This had been a period of great political and religious chaos brought on by continual fighting that scattered the people. As the Middle Ages ended, nation states in England, France, Spain, and Portugal began to emerge from the chaos.

European Exploration and Early Settlement

Between 1492 and 1550, Spain conquered more land than the Roman Empire had in five centuries. The empire that Spain created was the envy of the Western world. Other nations raced to create empires of their own.

Several factors inspired the European exploration and the colonization of present-day South Carolina. The most common motive was the desire for wealth, followed closely by the desire for land. Another reason for conquest was the desire to claim new territory. Religion was also a factor. The ambition to spread a particular religion or to find a haven free of religious persecution led some people to explore or settle the South Carolina coasts.

The colonization of America, and what is now South Carolina, took place in part because of the search for religious freedom. This sixteenth-century woodcut by Lucas Cranach depicts the Holy Communion of the Protestants, who broke free from the Catholic Church and came to America to escape religious persecution. Also shown here is imagery of Catholics riding to hell. Though the search for religious freedom was a major force in the colonization of America, other factors were involved as well. Europeans also colonized America in pursuit of wealth, land, and territory.

Spanish Exploration

Many people begin tracing the history of the colonization of South Carolina from the beginning of the first English colony in the mid-seventeenth century. However, the English were not the first European explorers to arrive in what is now South Carolina. That honor belongs to the Spanish, who "discovered" South Carolina about 150 years before the English set foot there.

Following Christopher Columbus's famous 1492 voyage to the Western Hemisphere, Spain claimed most of Central America and much of South America. The discovery of gold and silver in Mexico and Peru in the early 1500s partly led the Spanish to seek fortune farther north. Spain quickly claimed most of what is now the southeastern United States. They called this land La Florida.

In 1520 or 1521, a Spanish sea captain named Francisco Gordillo sailed along the coast of present-day South Carolina. Gordillo stopped to explore Winyah Bay. While there, he tricked Native Americans into coming aboard his ships. He did this by first capturing two Native Americans, bringing them aboard, and showering them with gifts.

The Spaniards then invited more Natives Americans onto their ships with the promise of similar gifts. Once the Native Americans were on board, Gordillo set sail for Santo Domingo (present-day Haiti), taking with him between 50 and 140 Native American prisoners.

One of Gordillo's Native American captives learned Spanish and grew close to the Spaniards. The Native American was given the name Francisco Chicora by the Spaniards. (Chicora was the Sioux name for the Carolina coast.) Chicora entertained the Spaniards with wild tales about his land. He told them of giants and of men and women with long tails who lived there. He also claimed that the land was rich with gold.

An important Spanish official named Lucas Vásquez de Ayllón was very interested in these fanciful tales. In fact, he was so inspired by them that he led a fleet of three ships back to Winyah Bay in 1526. On these ships were about 600 Spanish men, women, and children; African slaves; eighty-nine horses; and the equipment needed to start a colony.

The Spanish expeditions to the New World were the beginning of the colonization of what is now America. These expeditions were motivated by the search for riches in the southeastern part of today's America. Part of this search for riches involved the help, and often exploitation, of the native people. This is depicted in this 1591 painting by Theodore de Bry, which was part of his "Americae" series. De Bry's painting shows native people being used to carry the equipment of the Spanish explorers.

The colonists that Ayllón led to the New World first settled in an unknown location along the coast. They called the colony San Miguel de Gualdape. It was the first European settlement in what is now South Carolina.

The colony did not last long, however. As a result of disease and starvation, Ayllón was forced to move the colony to Winyah Bay, near present-day Georgetown. Unfortunately for the 600 or so settlers, this change in location did not help. Within a few months, two out of every three colonists, including Ayllón, had died. To make matters worse, Native Americans attacked the settlers, and the slaves they had brought with them revolted. The 150 surviving settlers quickly returned to the West Indies.

The Spanish maintained an on-and-off presence in today's South Carolina from the time of Ayllón's colonization in 1526 until they finally abandoned the region in 1587. Spanish explorer Hernando de Soto passed through the central part of today's South Carolina in 1540. The last settlement of the Spanish, known as Santa Elena, was probably the most important. This settlement, established in 1566 on what is now Parris Island, served as the capital of La Florida. However, when the Spanish abandoned Santa Elena in 1587, the land that would one day be known as South Carolina was once again left to the Native Americans until the English established a settlement there in 1670.

French Exploration

Although the Spanish claimed the land they called La Florida, not all nations recognized Spain's rights to it. The French were the first to challenge Spain's claim on the land that occupies today's South Carolina. In 1542, Giovanni da Verrazano, an Italian working for France, explored the eastern coast of what is now the United States. France then made several attempts to colonize the coastal region.

At that time, a group existed in France called the French Huguenots. The French Huguenots were Protestants who were being persecuted by France's Catholic-controlled government. A man named Gaspard de Coligny wanted to establish a refuge for the French Huguenots in the southeastern part of the present-day

Gaspard de Coligny, shown in this sixteenth-century portrait, was one of several Protestants who led a large number of French Huguenots to the New World. In an attempt to escape France's Catholic-controlled government, Coligny commissioned a man named Jean Ribault in 1562 to bring 150 French Huguenots to the New World. However, Ribault's colony proved unsuccessful. The French Huguenots failed to plant successful crops and soon ran out of food. They also failed to organize a firm governmental system. The French Huguenots finally abandoned their settlement in the spring of 1563.

United States. A Frenchman named Jean Ribault was commissioned to carry out Coligny's plans.

In February 1562, Ribault and 150 other Huguenots made the voyage from France to the New World. They briefly explored the mouth of St. John's River near modern-day Jacksonville, Florida, before sailing northward. When they reached what is now Parris Island, they built a fort. They named it Charlesfort and the region Carolus in honor of King Charles IX of France. Ribault named the waters around the fort Port Royal, and this is the name it still bears today.

As with the Spanish colonies, the French colony on present-day Parris Island was doomed from the start. After overseeing the initial layout of the settlement, Ribault went back to France for more settlers and supplies. He left behind twenty-seven men to continue the settlement in his absence.

Shown here in this 1591 engraving by Theodore de Bry, part of his "Americae" series, are French Huguenots arriving at a wide river they named Port Royal. In the engraving, the Huguenots sail up the river, where they encounter a group of Native Americans roasting a lynx. The Huguenots later named the area Lynx Point. Native Americans were central in helping the French Huguenots settle in South Carolina. With little food due to failed crops, the French Huguenots relied on natives for food to survive. Though the French colony ultimately failed, Native Americans helped the colony survive as long as it did.

These men struggled for survival. Failing to plant crops, the colonists soon ran out of food. Native Americans helped them by giving them food, but, soon after that, the strong house where the men kept their food and supplies burned to the ground. Native Americans again came to the aid of the settlers, helping them to rebuild it, but the men were already greatly discouraged.

In addition, the man whom Ribault left in charge, Captain Albert de la Pierria, was a tyrant. He banished a soldier named La Chère to a nearby deserted island. The colonists, angered by the cruel acts of their leader, killed him and rescued La Chère.

Ribault had planned to return to Charlesfort before the end of the year. However, he had been delayed by a religious war in France. After weeks of waiting for Ribault's return, the French colonists finally decided to abandon their colony in the spring of 1563. They cut down trees to build a boat and used shirts and bedsheets for sails.

The men set sail for France, but partway across the ocean, they ran out of food. Starving, the men ate their shoes and other leather items. When that was gone, they decided that one man should be killed and eaten so that the others could survive. La Chère was chosen. He was killed and eaten by the other men. Sources say that by the time the survivors of the voyage were rescued off the coast of England, they had lost their minds.

By 1587, present-day South Carolina was largely free of a European presence until the English landing of 1670. The only lasting legacies of Spanish and French colonization of the land were the place names of St. Helena (Spanish) and Port Royal (French). However, the failure of the Spanish and French colonies opened the way for English colonization, the first permanent European colonization in South Carolina.

CHAPTER 2

Although the English were latecomers in colonizing North America, it was they who achieved extraordinary success. In the 1600s, the English established thirteen colonies along the Atlantic coast.

The first successful colony to be established by the English was in Jamestown, Virginia, in 1607. Thirteen years later, the Pilgrims, a group of Protestants from England, sailed from England to the coast of Massachusetts. There they founded the Plymouth Colony.

The English Settlement of Charles Towne

Meanwhile, the king of England, Charles I, asserted England's claim to the land south of Virginia by granting the territory (later named Carolana, Latin for "Land of Charles") to Sir Robert Heath in 1629. Heath, however, eventually forfeited his charter.

In 1663, King Charles II changed the spelling of "Carolana" to "Carolina." That same year, he granted the colony to eight of his most loyal English noblemen. These men would become Carolina's lords proprietors, or landlords. They would remain in England and collect a small fee, called a quitrent, from those who wished to rent land from them. Those who wished to purchase land in Carolina also had to buy it from the proprietors.

The proprietors wanted to attract as many people to Carolina as they could. For this reason, they established the Fundamental Constitutions in 1669, which was partly authored by the political philosopher John Locke. Among other things, this frame of government offered settlers freedom of religion, something that was

Shown here is the Fundamental Constitutions of Carolina *(left)* and the man who initiated the English colonization of Carolina, King Charles II *(right)*. In granting the colony to eight noblemen in 1663, Charles II established a place for the English to go to begin business and practice whichever religion they wished. These freedoms were outlined in the Fundamental Constitutions and became central to the establishment of the American nation. See page 53 for the transcription.

hard to come by at that time. The cheap land and religious freedom attracted more than 100 people to sign up to be Carolina's first permanent settlers. Though the Fundamental Constitutions was an important document intended to serve as the framework for governing and settling South Carolina, it was never actually ratified and never served these purposes.

Three ships, the *Carolina*, the *Port Royal*, and the *Albemarle*, set sail from England for the New World in August 1669. During the voyage, however, the ships were slammed by terrible storms that wrecked the *Albemarle* and the *Port Royal*. Although no one was killed in these incidents, the storms delayed the trip.

The *Carolina* and another ship called the *Three Brothers* did not both reach the coast of present-day South Carolina until May 1670. Aboard these ships were 148 men and women. It had taken them more than half a year to complete their journey.

The proprietors had planned for the colonists to settle at Port Royal, in what is now southeastern South Carolina. However, they had not taken into account the fact that the area was already occupied by Native Americans.

Soon after arriving in the New World, the colonists were greeted by the Kiawah tribe. The Kiawahs told them of the bloodthirsty Westo tribe who lived in Port Royal, and urged them to settle instead at Kiawah. The colonists finally agreed that Port Royal was not only open to attack by the Westos but also by the Spaniards at St. Augustine. They headed north toward Kiawah.

In early April, the colonists settled about 10 miles (16 km) from the mouth of the Kiawah River on a high bluff they called Albemarle Point. After a year, the name of the town was changed to Charles Towne, in honor of England's king Charles II.

Learning from the Native Americans

After arriving in what is now South Carolina, the ship *Carolina* immediately returned to the West Indies to bring more settlers. Over the next few years, more and more English from both England and the West Indies moved to Charles Towne.

These early colonists planted corn, potatoes, and other crops, but the climate of Carolina was different from what they were used to. Failed crops resulted in food shortages. However, the colony was able to survive from techniques they learned from the Native Americans.

The settlers learned from the Native Americans how to keep insects from eating their crops. They also learned techniques for catching and preparing different kinds of game. The Native Americans taught the colonists many uses for a strange, hairlike plant that the early French settlers called Spanish beard. This plant, which hung from every tree along the coastal area, was used to fill mattresses and pillows. It was also mixed with mud to make chimneys stronger and to fill the cracks between the logs in cabins.

By the late 1600s, settlers began to trade with the Native Americans. They gave them tools, rum, and guns in exchange for deerskins and animal furs. The furs were then shipped to and sold in England, where they were especially valuable.

A Permanent Home

In 1680, ten years after the colonists landed in present-day South Carolina, they moved the location of Charles Towne. Albemarle Point had been deemed unhealthy because of its swamps. The colonists had begun looking for a new site only three years after the original landing.

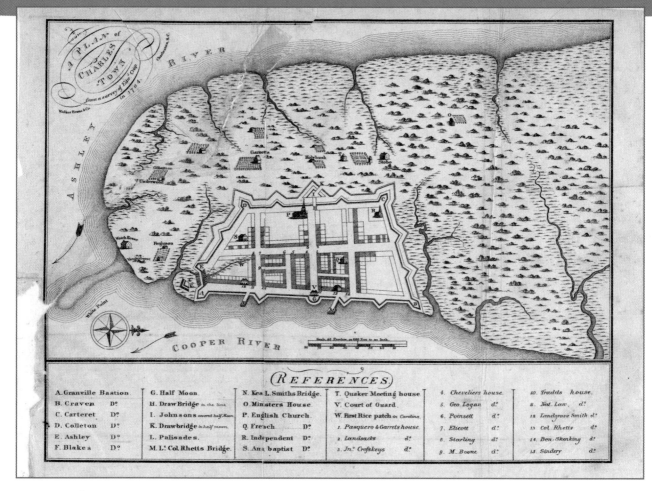

A PLAN of CHARLES TOWN from a survey of Edw. Crisp in 1704.

(REFERENCES)

A. Granville Bastion	G. Half Moon.	N. Kea L. Smiths Bridge.	T. Quaker Meeting house.	4. Cheveliers house.	10. Tradds house.
B. Craven D°	H. Draw Bridge in the line.	O. Minsters House.	V. Court of Guard.	5. Geo. Logan d°	11. Nat. Law. d°
C. Carteret D°	I. Johnsons covered half Moon.	P. English Church.	W. First Rice patch in Carolina.	6. Poinsett d°	12. Landgrave Smith d°
D. Colleton D°	K. Drawbridge in half moon.	Q. French D°	1. Pasquero & Garrets house.	7. Elicott d°	13. Col. Rhetts d°
E. Ashley D°	L. Palisades.	R. Independent D°	2. Landsacks d°	8. Starling d°	14. Ben. Skenking d°
F. Blakes D°	M. L. Col. Rhetts Bridge.	S. Ana baptist D°	3. Jn° Crofskeys d°	9. M. Boone d°	15. Sindery d°

As one of the earliest examples of urban planning in the New World, Charles Towne, shown here, was designed for a society that provided many freedoms. With a large town square for the militia to perform drills, the English colony was essentially claiming its independence from the old country and by preparing to fight its own battles. With these open spaces, the town allowed for public offices and churches where Protestantism could be practiced freely, as well as any other religion.

They decided on a site called Oyster Point, which stretched between the Etiwan and the Kiawah rivers. This land was considered to be healthier, easier to defend, and better for trade. In July 1672, the surveyor general for the colony, John Culpeper, began laying out a town at Oyster Point.

The town was originally called New Charles Towne. However, once everyone from the old site had moved there, "New" was dropped from the name. The town was now known as Charles Towne. It would eventually be renamed again, this time as Charleston, in 1783.

Later, in honor of Ashley Cooper, the lord proprietor who had written the Fundamental Constitutions of Carolina with the assistance of John Locke, the Kiawah River was renamed the Ashley River and the Etiwan River was renamed the Cooper River.

The layout of Charles Towne was grand. The city had wide streets, and a large town square was left open to allow the militia to perform its drills. Around the square, lots had been designated for public offices and for a church with a graveyard. Soon Charles Towne was one of America's most successful towns, and South Carolina was on its way to becoming one of the wealthiest of the thirteen colonies.

CHAPTER 3

The 1700s was a time of great prosperity for the colony of South Carolina. During that time, the colony of South Carolina was full of human variety and very accepting of religious diversity. South Carolina also experienced many cultural and theatrical "firsts" in the 1700s. Its residents were able to enjoy concerts and theatrical performances, and those who missed them were able to read about these events in the colony's very own newspaper.

A Flourishing Colony

The 1700s also saw the emergence of cash-producing crops in South Carolina. By 1760, Charles Towne was the richest town in the thirteen colonies. In 1763, a man named Dr. George Milligen-Johnston wrote the book *A Short Description of the Province of South-Carolina*. In his book, he described South Carolina as not only the richest colony in the New World but perhaps the most successful settlement in the whole world.

Among other things, the Fundamental Constitutions opened up South Carolina to people of many different religions. Although some people today may take religious freedom for granted, the freedom to worship as one chose was hard to come by in colonial times.

South Carolina, however, was ahead of its time. From the beginning, the colony welcomed people of various religions. In contrast, many of the other colonies banned or persecuted Quakers and Jews, as well as any other people who did not belong to the Church of England. Many historians believe that the

[43]

CHAP. V.

Of the Diseases most frequent in Charles-town and its Neighbourhood.

SECTION I.

THE Diseases, that may be termed Epide-mics, are either acute or chronic : The acute Diseases may be subdivided into those of the warm and those of the cold Seasons.

The first are Intermittents of all Kinds, Flux-es, and Cholera Morbus : The Winter Diseases are Pleurisies, Peripneumonies, and Catarrhal Fevers.

The Chronic Diseases are Obstructions of the Abdominal Viscera, Hæmorrhoids, Ruptures, Worm-fevers, and what is called the Lame Dis-temper.

* Intermittents appear in different Forms, such as Tertian, Double-tertian, Quotidian, and Remitting Fevers ; all which, however they may vary in their Type, in different Constitu-tions and other Circumstances, are, neverthe-

* Vid. *Pringle*'s Observations on the Diseases of the Ar-my, and *Cleghorn*'s Diseases of *Minorca*.

F 2   less,

In his book *A Short Description of the Province of South-Carolina*, Dr. George Milligen-Johnston captured the essence of the colony's new prosperity. In this book, one of the first accounts of South Carolina colony life, Milligen-Johnston describes not only the prosperity of the colony, but also such details as the weather and diseases, as described on the page above. See page 53 for a transcription.

religious tolerance of the colony of South Carolina was surpassed only by that of Rhode Island.

By the mid-1700s, there were enough Jews in Charles Towne for them to form their own congregation. Kahal Kadosh Beth Elohim (Holy Congregational House of God) was established in 1749 and is today one of the oldest ongoing Jewish congregations in the United States.

The colony of South Carolina was also home to people of many different nationalities. At first, nearly all the South Carolina colonists came from England. However, as early as the 1680s, immigrants from many different countries started coming to what is now South Carolina.

In 1682, a Scottish man named Henry Erskine (also called Lord Cardross) prepared to obtain a tract of land in South Carolina. In 1684, he led about 150 Scots to the colony. They established a community just south of where Beaufort, South Carolina, stands today. Although the town was destroyed in 1686 by a Spanish invasion, many more Scottish people continued to migrate to South Carolina.

The French Huguenots finally began colonizing South Carolina in great numbers in the 1680s. The Huguenots built a settlement called Jamestown just north of Charles Towne along the banks of the Santee River.

Although this settlement did not last, the French, too, continued to grow in number in South Carolina. By the mid-1700s, only a little more than half the population was of English origin. The rest was a mixture of Scots-Irish, French, German, and other nationalities. Because of the area's reliance on slavery, there was also a large black population in South Carolina. By the 1760s, about 60,000 of the colony's approximately 100,000 inhabitants were black.

One example of the religious freedoms enjoyed by the colonists were Jewish synagogues. One of them was the Kahal Kadosh Beth Elohim (Holy Congregational House of God), which is shown here. With enough Jews in Charles Towne in the mid-1700s to build their own congregation, a strong Jewish presence established itself in South Carolina.

Around 1730, Eleazer Phillips founded the colony's first newspaper, the *South Carolina Weekly Journal*. Although it lasted only half a year, it was quickly followed by the appearance of the *South-Carolina Gazette* in 1732. This newspaper lasted for about half a century. Among its other achievements, the *South-Carolina Gazette* was the first newspaper in America to have a female publisher. Elizabeth Timothy achieved this status in 1739 upon the death of her husband, Lewis Timothy, who had been running the paper. She ran the paper for eight years, until her son took over when he turned twenty-one.

Charles Towne could boast of many cultural firsts taking place in the city. The first opera presented in America, *Flora, or Hob in the Well*, was held in Charles Towne in 1735. Charles Towne was also the site of the first true playhouse. On February 12, 1736, the New Theater opened. The first play performed in the theater was *The Recruiting Officer*, a comedy about an army recruiter in England. Though the original theater no longer exists, a new theater, known as the Dock Street Theater, now stands in its place.

In 1762, the St. Cecelia Society was formed, and it sponsored America's first symphony orchestra. Charles Towne was also the site of the first public museum in America. In 1773, the Charles

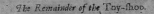

One of the major signs of a community's success is the establishment of a lasting newspaper. The *South-Carolina Gazette*, an early edition of which is shown here, was the second of Charles Towne's papers, but the first successful one. The *South-Carolina Gazette* lasted for about half a century. Included in the paper were, what we would call today letters to the editor, in which ordinary citizens had a voice in the community. In these letters, citizens gave their opinions about a variety of topics important to the colony. See page 54 for a transcription.

Towne Library Society founded the Charles Towne Museum, which is still in operation today.

Rice and Indigo

Nearly all of the first colonists to arrive in South Carolina were farmers. They raised cattle and grew tobacco and corn. For its first few years, however, the colony lacked a big moneymaking crop. This changed when rice was introduced to the colony in the late 1680s.

Along with rice, indigo became a cash crop for South Carolina after Eliza Lucas (later Eliza Pinckney) successfully grew the indigo crop in 1742. It was previously believed that indigo could not be grown in the colonies. Shown here is an illustration in the corner of a map of South Carolina depicting a man extracting the blue dye from the indigo crop. The fact that indigo processing was shown on a map of South Carolina is a testament of how important the crop was to the colony.

How rice was introduced to the colony is still a subject of debate. What is known for certain is that by 1700, farmers near South Carolina's coast, namely West African slaves, were successfully growing rice, and it was fast becoming the colony's most important crop. The rice that was not eaten by the South Carolinians was sold to the other colonies, to England, and to the West Indies. By the 1730s, South Carolina was exporting an average of over 20 million pounds of rice, and it was bringing tremendous wealth to the colony.

In 1739, seventeen-year-old Eliza Lucas, later Eliza Pinckney, began developing a second major money-making crop for South Carolina—indigo. Indigo is a plant from which blue dye is made. In colonial times, there were no artificial dyes. To dye cloth, people had to extract colors from plants. One of the most valuable colors in colonial times was blue. This was perhaps because it was the hardest color to produce a dye for. For many years, only kings and queens wore blue.

Indigo had long been grown in India and Egypt, but it was not introduced into Europe until the fifteenth century. Before South Carolina began growing the plant, England had obtained a similar blue dye from another plant. The climate of South Carolina was favorable for growing indigo. However, several colonists had attempted to grow the plant without success. This all changed when Lucas began experimenting with growing indigo on her family's plantation on Wappoo Creek. After years of effort and several failures, Lucas finally raised a successful indigo crop in 1742. The news quickly spread, and indigo soon joined rice as a booming South Carolina farm product.

Rice and indigo brought great prosperity, but raising these crops required a lot of workers who would be able to labor in the

TO BE SOLD on *Wednesday* the 21st of this Instant, a choice Parcel of Slaves, imported in the Ship *Berkley Galley*, Peregrine Stockdale Commander, from *Angola* directly, by *Jenys & Baker*.

Though indigo proved to be one of the crops that made South Carolina a successful colony, the processing of indigo often led to harsh measures, as shown in this newspaper advertisement for the sale of slaves. Slaves were often put to work to harvest and process crops for the colonists. Slaves in South Carolina were often from Africa, but they also included Native Americans who were bought and sold as commodities.

fields under the blazing hot summer sun. For this reason, Africans were brought to the colonies and put to work as slaves.

Slavery was legal in South Carolina from the start, and the colony had more slaves than any other. However, Africans were not the only people who were enslaved. Traders found it profitable to round up Native Americans and sell them into slavery as well.

The colonists of South Carolina were the leading slave traders of Native Americans in the New World. Some of the Native Americans were bought by South Carolinians, but, more often, they were shipped to the West Indies and sold there.

Rice and indigo helped to make many plantation owners rich, and South Carolina enjoyed a prosperity that lasted until the colonial times ended with the start of the Revolutionary War in 1775.

CHAPTER 4

Although people had referred to South Carolina and North Carolina separately since about 1690, they were still both technically part of a larger region known as Carolina. Because of its wealth, South Carolina dominated poorer North Carolina. Even the lords proprietors favored South Carolina over its northern counterpart. Finally, in 1712, the Carolina colony was formally divided into two parts, North Carolina and South Carolina. They officially became separate colonies of England in 1729.

Pirates, Rebellion, and War

Although the 1700s were prosperous years for South Carolinians, they were also filled with threats from both land and sea. Threats from land came from angry Native Americans who had been mistreated. Threats from the sea came from greedy pirates.

The 1700s were also a time of rebellion. The South Carolinians experienced many rebellious uprisings from the Africans they forced to work in their fields. The colonists themselves even rebelled against the proprietors whom they felt unsatisfactorily governed their lives.

In 1707, the South Carolina colony had granted Native Americans the land between the Combahee and Savannah rivers. However, as more settlers came to South Carolina and the colonies grew, the settlers began taking lands that belonged to the Native Americans. This made Native American tribes, like the Yemassee, very angry. They were also unhappy with the deceitful business practices of South Carolina traders.

In April 1715, the Yemassees attacked the settlers in the Beaufort area, killing about 100 people. Soon the Creeks and other southeastern tribes, such as the Catawbas, joined the Yemassees in their quest to rid the area of European settlers.

Settlers from the outskirts of the colony flooded into Charles Towne, which soon resembled a fortress. For a short period, the Native Americans even managed to confine the colonists to the town.

Finally, the Cherokees joined forces with the colonists in January 1716. Fear of the Cherokees caused many of the smaller tribes to seek peace, while the Yemassees fled to Florida.

Though the Yemassee war had ended, it took a heavy toll on South Carolina. The war caused such fear in the hearts of colonists that it took nearly ten years for resettlement to occur in many areas.

Pirates

Pirates were a problem for the colonists of South Carolina because they robbed ships along the coast. Not only did ship owners suffer from piracy, but the merchants and planters whose goods were stolen suffered as well.

One pirate in particular, Edward "Blackbeard" Teach, was quite well-known and feared. Blackbeard got his name from his habit of braiding his long, black beard and tying it with colorful ribbons. Between 1717 and 1718, Blackbeard harassed many ships sailing along the coasts of Virginia, Delaware, and the Carolinas.

Another pirate who terrorized ships along the Carolina coastline was Stede Bonnet. He was known as the Gentleman Pirate because of his manners and dress. Although he had a nickname that made him sound harmless, Bonnet was every bit as cruel as Blackbeard. In fact, he is believed to have invented the practice of making his victims walk the plank, or jump to their deaths from a plank placed over the edge of a ship.

Being distant from the rich nations in Europe that had powerful militaries, the colonies were vulnerable to all sorts of dangers including piracy. One of the most famous pirates who terrorized South Carolina was Edward "Blackbeard" Teach. Blackbeard, shown here in this 1724 engraving, is in full costume, heavily armed, and holding a saber. Blackbeard, along with other pirates such as Stede Bonnet, terrorized and robbed ships along the South Carolina coast. As a testament of its growing independence, the colony soon took a stand against piracy. In September 1718, Governor Robert Johnson hunted down and captured Bonnet and many in his crew. It was a move toward military independence for the colony.

Blackbeard the Pirate.

In an incident that took place in 1718, Blackbeard's actions finally convinced the people of South Carolina that piracy must end. Blackbeard sailed four ships into the water off the coast of Charles Towne. On these ships were more than 400 pirates. The pirates robbed eight or nine vessels that were coming from or going to Charles Towne Harbor and took the passengers and crews hostage. Blackbeard then sent a message to Robert Johnson, governor of South Carolina, stating that unless his demands were met, he would kill the hostages.

Blackbeard was not after the usual gold. He wanted medicine for sick members of his crew. The city sent a chest of medicine out to Blackbeard, and he retreated to North Carolina after releasing his hostages.

Over the months following the incident with Blackbeard, Virginians and South Carolinians worked to stamp out piracy. In September 1718, Governor Johnson sent Colonel William Rhett to hunt down pirates. Rhett led a small fleet into North Carolina waters where he battled with Stede Bonnet and his crew for about five hours. When the battle was over, Bonnet and a number of his crew members had been captured.

Although Bonnet made a futile attempt to escape, he and his men were hanged in Charles Towne a few months later. A Virginia expedition took care of Blackbeard. After a fierce battle between Blackbeard and Lieutenant Robert Maynard of the British navy, Blackbeard and about ten of his men lay dead. The rest of Blackbeard's men were taken to Virginia where they were tried and hanged.

Rebellion Against the Proprietors

The lords proprietors who had been appointed by King Charles II had total control over the political and financial lives of the colonists. The proprietors from England ran the colony to suit themselves, and the people had little to say about their own government. The proprietors also failed to protect the colonists during invasions and war. The colonists had successfully protected themselves against attacks by the Yemassees and raids by pirates with little help from the powerful proprietors. The colonists were also angry about the quitrent, an estate tax they had to pay the proprietors. And finally, England managed to suppress religious liberty in 1704. Religious liberty was not reestablished in South Carolina until 1706.

King George I, shown in this nineteenth-century portrait by Hermann Goldschmidt, was one of the early saviors of the South Carolina colony. Taken advantage of by the lords proprietors, many South Carolinians fought to be freed from their proprietors' rule. This meant, however, that England would have to get involved. George I eventually bought back the proprietors' shares and owned the rights to the colony.

In 1719, many South Carolinians signed a petition asking that they be removed from the proprietors' rule. The South Carolina leaders met at a convention and elected a new governor, James Moore Jr., to replace Robert Johnson, who had been set in place by the proprietors. The convention sent word to England asking that South Carolina be made a royal colony. This would mean that the colony would be protected and governed by the British crown. King George I granted their request, making South Carolina a royal colony.

Britain ruled the colony but allowed the colonists to govern themselves. In 1729, the British government paid a large sum of money to the proprietors, officially buying out their rights to South Carolina.

126. Journal of the Commons House of Assembly

The 10 day of Novemb^r. 1739

M^r. Mazyck from the Commee appointed to consider of proper means to relieve the People about Stono from the dangers arising from domestic Enemys: who was also appointed a Comee to consider of, and to Report to this House, the most effectual means for prevention of such dangers throughout the Province, made a Report which he first read in his place, and then delivered it in at the Table. And the same was again afterwards read to the House, and is in the Words following (that is to say

Report of the Comee appointed to consider of the most effectual means to prevent the dangers arising from Domestic Enemys.

The Commee appointed to consider of proper means to releeve the People about Stono from the dangers arising from domestic Enemys; and to consider of the most effectual means for prevention of such dangers throughout the Province.

Report. Whereas by the late unhappy accident at Stono it appears to be absolutely necessary to get a sufficient number of white Persons into this Province: The Commee beg leave to recommend that a Bill may be brought in for that purpose to the following Effect.

1. That every Person owning or intitled to any Slaves in this Province, for every 10 Male Slaves above the age of 12 Years, shall be obliged to find and provide one able white Man for the Militia of this Province who shall be subject to appear in the Militia, and do all the Dutys required by the Militia Laws of this Province.

2. That any Person owning or claiming any Lands in this Province, over and above the quantity of 4000 Acres, and under the quantity of 20,000 Acres, shall be obliged to find and provide one able white Man, to serve in the Militia; for every 2000 Acres of Land over the said quantity of 4000 Acres, and under the said quantity of 20,000 Acres, so owned or claimed by such Persons. And for every 5000 Acres over and above the said quantity of 20,000 Acres, one able white Man to serve in the Militia of this Province; over and besides the number of white Men such Persons are obliged to furnish for the Militia as aforesaid, for or by reason or on account of their Slaves as aforesaid.

3. That every Owner of such Lands and Slaves as aforesaid, who shall be deficient herein, his Sons and Apprentices above the Age of sixteen Years and under the Age of sixty Years be accounted for and taken as so many of such White Persons to serve in the Militia as aforesaid.

4. That every Person who shall refuse or neglect to comply with the terms aforesaid shall forfeit & pay the sum of 6£ per Month for every Male white Servant or white Man they shall want to serve in the Militia, required as afsd for the quantity of Lands & Slaves held or claimed by them in this Province.

5. That the Moneys arising

755

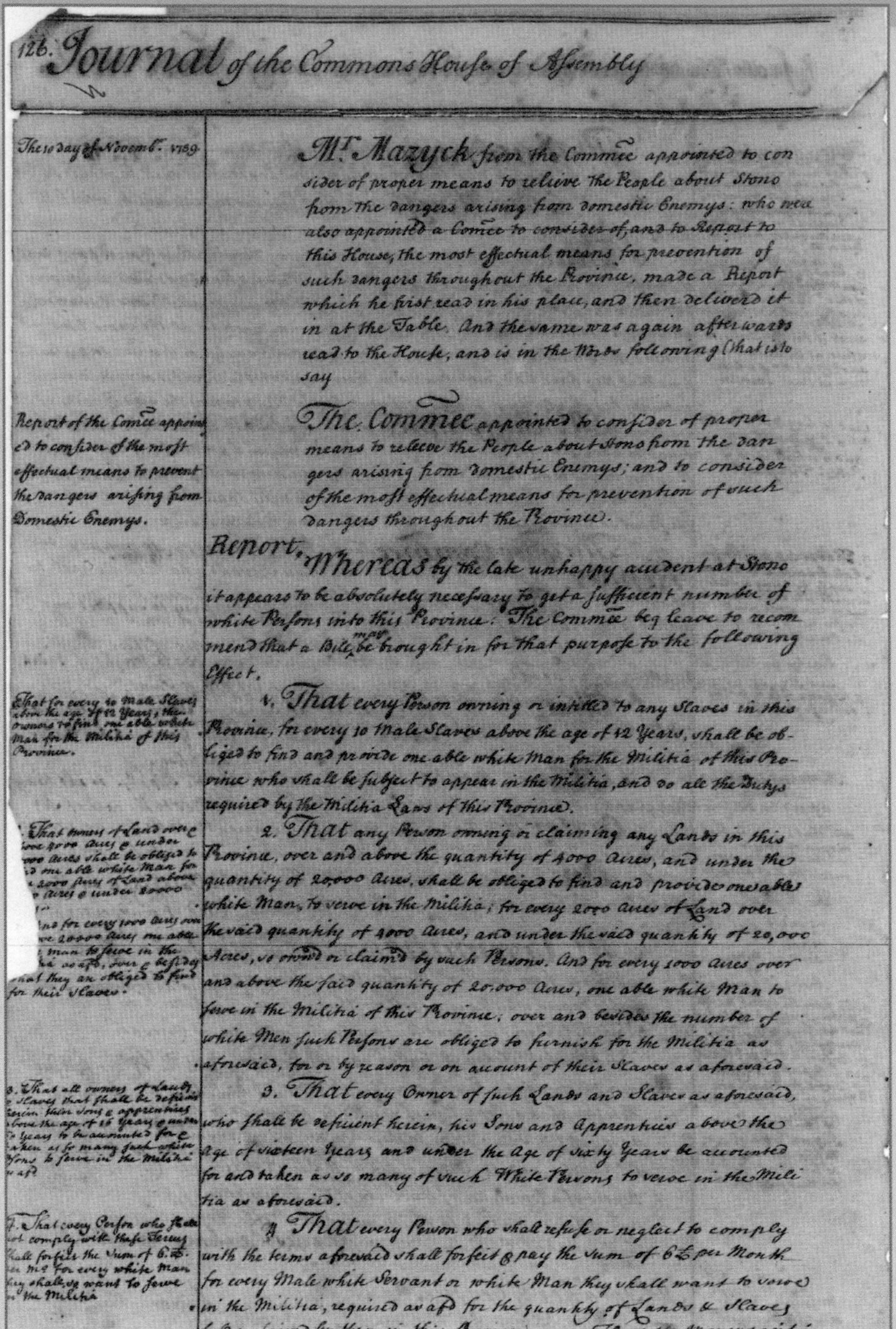

Shown here is a 1739 entry into the *Journal of the Commons House of Assembly* outlining measures to be taken to prevent another insurrection like the Stono Rebellion. This eventually came to be the Slave Code of 1740, which forbade slaves to do such things as assemble in groups, own livestock, or learn to read. There were other laws, though, that were created to avoid another uprising. Such laws included making the slave workday no longer than fourteen to fifteen hours and forbidding the murdering of slaves. See page 54 for a transcription.

The Stono Rebellion

By about 1708, African slaves outnumbered the colonists in South Carolina. The harsh conditions and treatment of the slaves led to numerous runaways and rebellions.

By the late 1730s, relations between Spain and England were also very bad. Spain, in an attempt to hurt England's southern colonies, announced that it would grant freedom to any slaves who escaped to St. Augustine. The slaves, inspired by rumors of the announcement, planned their escapes. By mid-1739, a few slaves had managed to escape to Florida and others hoped to follow.

Then, on Sunday, September 9, 1739, the slaves cleverly planned a revolt following a yellow fever epidemic that had killed many in the Charles Towne area. Word had also recently reached South Carolina that Spain and England were at war over shipping at sea, a conflict that began when a British sea captain claimed that a member of the Spanish coast guard had severed his ear. This was later called the War of Jenkin's Ear. The slave revolt may have also been triggered by the forthcoming Security Act, a law that would require all white males to carry weapons with them when they attended church. On the day of the rebellion, the white population was weak with disease, threatened by war, and unarmed because it was the Sabbath.

About 20 slaves broke into a store at Stono Bridge about 20 miles (32 km) southwest of Charles Towne. They murdered the store owners and stole firearms. Then they marched down the street yelling "Liberty!" Along the way, more slaves joined the rebellion until they numbered as many as 100. They traveled from house to house, killing men, women, and children and setting fire to plantations.

By late Sunday afternoon, a group of white planters with guns attacked the slaves as they stopped to rest in a field. A small battle ensued. The fighting ended with the death of at least fourteen slaves. Most of those who escaped were hunted down within a few weeks. They were later shot or hanged.

By the time the Stono Rebellion, as the uprising came to be known, was completely crushed, thirty whites and perhaps twice as many blacks had been killed. It was by far the largest and bloodiest incident of its kind in colonial America.

Following the Stono Rebellion, the Slave Code of 1740 was passed very quickly. The 1740 code forbade slaves to assemble in groups, own livestock, and learn to read.

Other laws were intended to benefit the slaves so that they would be less likely to attempt another rebellion. It became illegal to work a slave for more than fifteen hours per day in some seasons and more than fourteen in others. It became a crime for a master to kill a slave, which was punishable by a stiff fine.

The French and Indian War

As English colonists moved farther into the heartland of America, they began encroaching on the borders of New France. New France included most of the middle section of the present-day United States and stretched southward to the Gulf of Mexico. Britain's infringement upon France's claimed territory caused tension between the French and the English.

In 1752, a group of Ottawa and Ojibwa warriors were led by Charles Langlade, a French trader, to a British trading post where they killed thirteen Native Americans who had sided with the British. This was the first of many skirmishes that would eventually lead to the infamous French and Indian War (1754–1763).

Above is the muster roll and pay list for Colonel George Gabriel's company in the French and Indian War. This list tallied who was fighting and how much each person got paid. The French and Indian War was one of the few times during the colonization period when the American colonists and the English worked together, in this case fighting against the French. See page 55 for a transcription.

The French and Indian War was a bloody battle that was fought over most of North America. Although no major battles occurred in South Carolina, hundreds of South Carolinians helped the English win the war. By the end of the war in 1763, New France had fallen to the British. The American colonists and the British had worked together to defeat France, but they would soon be fighting each other.

CHAPTER 5

The American Revolution

With the victory of the French and Indian War, England emerged as the dominant power in North America. However, this success came at a cost. The war had left England almost bankrupt.

In order to make up for some of its debt, England started heavily taxing the thirteen colonies. Between 1764 and 1773, the British parliament taxed the colonists on many items, such as paper, glass, and tea.

The first tax that outraged the colonists was the Stamp Act of 1765. This act put a tax on all papers and documents. Special stamps were to be purchased by the colonists and affixed to all newspapers, legal documents, and even playing cards. The colonists protested the Stamp Act in newspaper articles, in speeches, in meetings, and even in riots.

Many colonies formed groups that were part of an organization called the Sons of Liberty, or the Liberty Boys. Charles Towne's Sons of Liberty branch often met beneath a huge oak tree, known as the Liberty Tree. There they spoke out angrily against British injustice.

When a ship carrying stamps for South Carolina arrived in Charles Towne, the Sons of Liberty, along with more than 2,000 people, participated in burning a dummy that was made to look like a hanged stamp collector. The British officials got the message.

When the Stamp Act finally went into effect in November 1765, South Carolina stopped the operation of its civil courts and

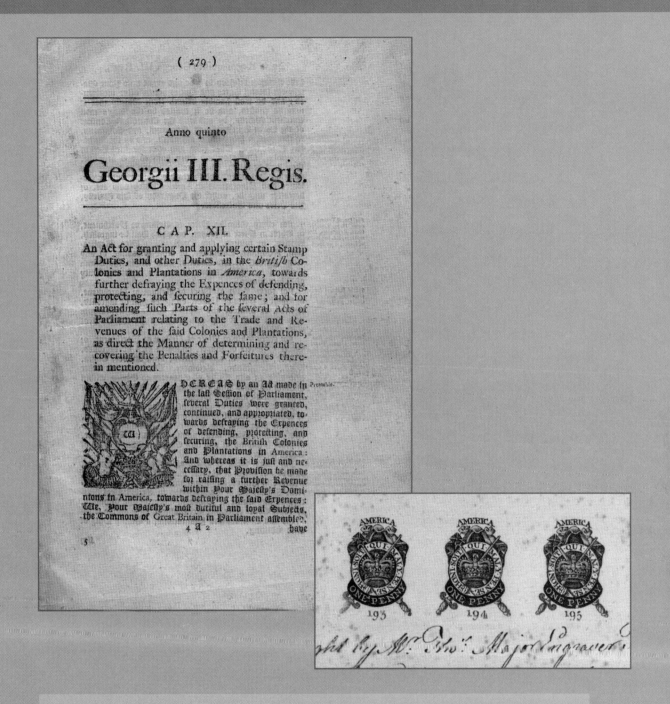

The French and Indian War cost England so much money that the nation was forced into conflict again, this time with the colonists, when it tried to recoup that lost money through the Stamp Act of 1765. The Stamp Act notice *(left)* taxed the colonists on a wide variety of legal and official documents, as well as products like playing cards. One-penny stamps *(right)* were used on newspapers, pamphlets, and all other papers of a certain size to tax the colonists. See page 55 for a transcription.

the *South-Carolina Gazette*. Other colonies took similar actions. Realizing the law was a failure, British lawmakers repealed the Stamp Act in March 1766. However, this was only the beginning of the fight between England and the colonies.

Soon after the Stamp Act was repealed, the British parliament passed the Townshend Acts. The Townshend Acts put taxes on certain goods such as paint, lead, glass, paper, and tea that were brought into the colonies. When colonists refused to buy British goods, Parliament, in 1770, removed all taxes except those placed on tea.

On December 16, 1773, during the infamous Boston Tea Party, protesters in Massachusetts dumped about 340 chests of English tea into the Boston Harbor in rebellion against the manipulation of the tax on tea. The British punished them by closing the port of Boston, putting many people out of work, and causing food shortages in the town due to the lack of imports. However, the other colonies came to the aid of the Massachusetts colony, sending food and other goods. South Carolina sent its most prized food product—rice.

In response to the Tea Act and the closing of the Boston port, American leaders decided to meet. This First Continental Congress was held in 1774 from September 5 to October 26 in Philadelphia, Pennsylvania. Every colony but Georgia sent delegates. South Carolina's delegates were Christopher Gadsden, Thomas Lynch, Henry Middleton, and brothers John and Edward Rutledge.

This First Continental Congress was the seed from which the United States Congress later grew. The First Continental Congress sent letters to England asking that the Tea Act be

Edward Rutledge

Chris Gadsden

Edward Rutledge *(left)* and Christopher Gadsden *(right)* were among South Carolina's delegates who responded to the Tea Act. They took part in the First Continental Congress held from September 5 to October 26, 1774, in Philadelphia, Pennsylvania. This First Continental Congress marked the beginning of the colonies' formation as a truly independent nation. The Revolutionary War, the ultimate fight for independence, soon followed.

repealed and that the punishment of Boston cease. The Congress also told the colonies to prepare for war with England.

Congress was right to prepare for war. England not only stood its ground but also sent British troops to destroy munitions. On April 19, 1775, the British troops were met by about seventy-five militiamen in Lexington, Massachusetts, and a fight ensued. This battle marked the beginning of the Revolutionary War, which lasted from 1775 to 1783.

South Carolina Becomes a State

In 1775, South Carolina formed a new government called the Provincial Congress. After learning of battles in Massachusetts, it began assembling troops to fight the English if necessary. Its members also signed a pledge stating that they were ready to sacrifice their fortunes and their lives for the good of America.

On May 10, 1775, the Second Continental Congress was held. This Congress made a last-ditch effort to make peace with King George III of England. It sent him a document called the Olive Branch Petition in which they explained their hope that harmony could be restored between England and the colonies. The petition was rejected.

War continued as the colonies moved toward independence. In January 1776, New Hampshire became the first of the thirteen colonies to create a state government that was completely free of British rule. South Carolina's Provincial Congress followed suit on March 26, 1776, when it adopted a state constitution and elected its first president, John Rutledge.

The first of more than 100 Revolutionary War battles to be fought on South Carolina soil took place in a town called Ninety Six from November 19 to 21, 1775. The fight was between 600 South Carolinian patriots, or Whigs (those fighting for independence from England), and 1,800 South Carolinian Loyalists, or Tories, (those who were remaining loyal to England and her rule over the colonies).

One of the major goals of the British was to capture Charles Towne. From there they felt they could move north and conquer other colonies. In May 1776, British ships sailed toward Charles Towne. In order to defend the capital, Colonel William Moultrie built a fort on Sullivans Island, which lay at the entrance to Charles Towne Harbor. Because the island had an abundance of palmetto trees, Moultrie used them to build the walls of the fort, which would later become known as Fort Moultrie.

The palmetto logs would prove to be a good defense against the British, who attacked on June 28, 1776. When the British fired upon the fort, their cannonballs were harmlessly absorbed into the logs. Colonel Moultrie returned cannon fire, doing much damage to the British fleet and killing many. After unsuccessfully pounding the fort with cannonballs for about twelve hours, the British finally gave up.

This failed British attempt to seize Charles Towne would keep them from attacking South Carolina until 1780. Because the palmetto logs held up so well during Britain's attack on Fort Moultrie, South Carolina was nicknamed the Palmetto State, and pictures of the tree were placed on the state flag and seal.

The Vote for Independence

Shortly after the battle at Fort Moultrie, the Continental Congress met to decide if the colonies would declare themselves independent from Great Britain. Each colony had a vote,

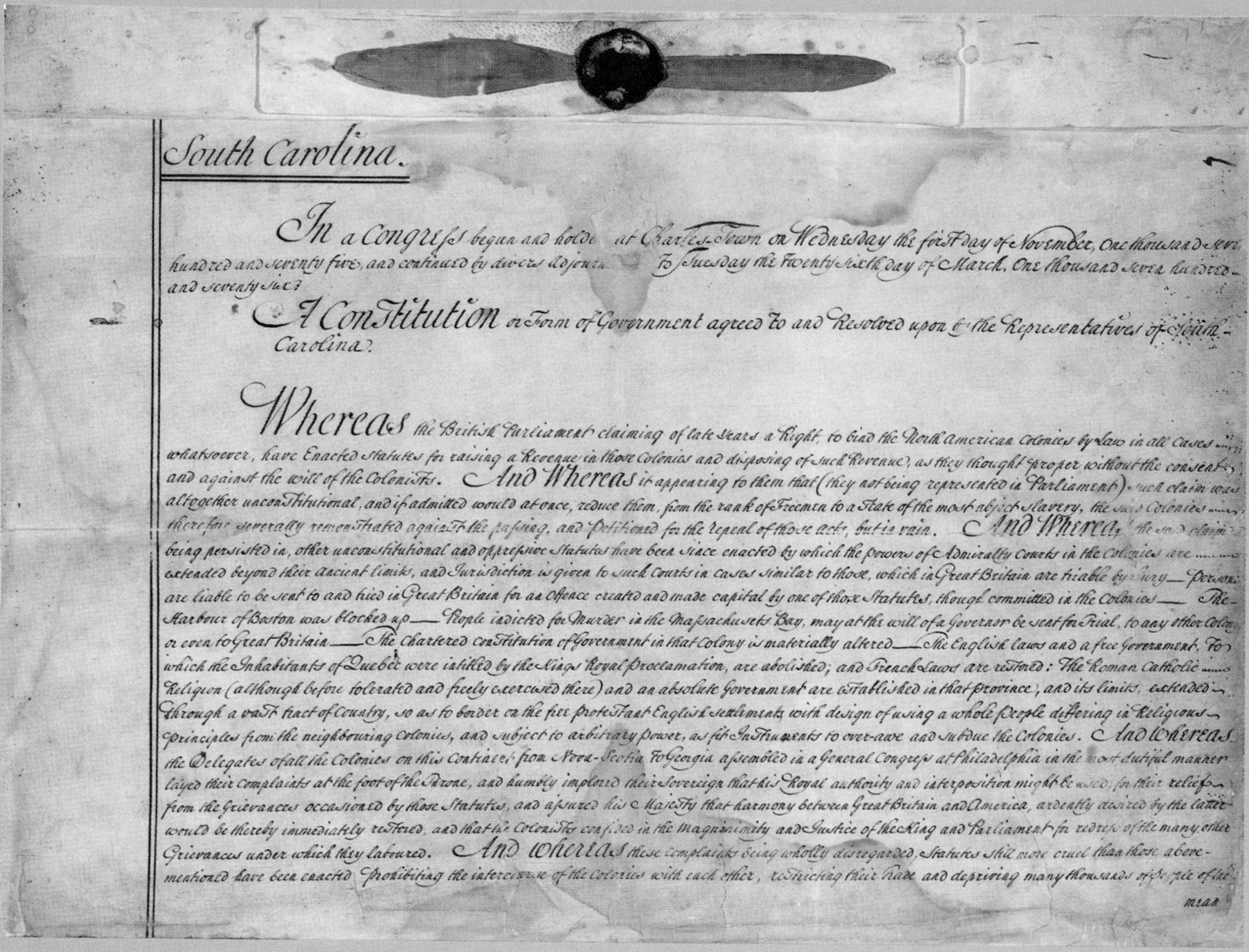

South Carolina.

In a Congress begun and holden at Charles-Town on Wednesday the first day of November, One thousand seven hundred and seventy five, and continued by divers Adjournments to Tuesday the Twenty sixth day of March, One thousand seven hundred and seventy six:

A Constitution or Form of Government agreed to and Resolved upon by the Representatives of South-Carolina.

Whereas the British Parliament claiming of late years a Right, to bind the North American Colonies by Law in all Cases whatsoever, have Enacted Statutes for raising a Revenue in those Colonies and disposing of such Revenue, as they thought proper without the consent, and against the will of the Colonists. And Whereas it appearing to them that (they not being represented in Parliament) such claim was altogether unconstitutional, and if admitted would at once, reduce them, from the rank of Freemen to a State of the most abject Slavery, the said Colonies therefore severally remonstrated against the passing, and Petitioned for the repeal of those Acts, but in vain. And Whereas the said claim being persisted in, other unconstitutional and oppressive Statutes have been since enacted by which the powers of Admiralty Courts in the Colonies are extended beyond their Ancient limits, and Jurisdiction is given to such Courts in cases similar to those, which in Great Britain are triable by Jury — Persons are liable to be sent to and tried in Great Britain for an Offence created and made capital by one of those Statutes, though committed in the Colonies — The Harbour of Boston was blocked up — People indicted for Murder in the Massachusets Bay, may at the will of a Governor be sent for Trial, to any other Colony or even to Great Britain — The Chartered Constitution of Government in that Colony is materially altered — The English laws and a free Government, to which the Inhabitants of Quebec were intitled by the Kings Royal Proclamation, are abolished; and French Laws are restored: The Roman Catholic Religion (although before tolerated and freely exercised there) and an absolute Government are established in that province; and its limits, extended through a vast tract of Country, so as to border on the free protestant English settlements with design of using a whole People differing in Religious principles from the neighbouring Colonies, and subject to arbitrary power, as fit Instruments to over-awe and subdue the Colonies. And Whereas the Delegates of all the Colonies on this Continent from Nova-Scotia to Georgia assembled in a General Congress at Philadelphia in the most dutiful manner layed their Complaints at the foot of the Throne, and humbly implored their Sovereign that his Royal authority and interposition might be used, for their relief from the Grievances occasioned by those Statutes, and assured his Majesty that harmony between Great Britain and America, ardently desired by the latter would be thereby immediately restored, and that the Colonists confided in the Magnanimity and Justice of the King and Parliament for redress of the many other Grievances under which they laboured. And Whereas these complaints being wholly disregarded, Statutes still more cruel than those above-mentioned have been enacted prohibiting the intercourse of the Colonies with each other, restricting their trade and depriving many thousands of people of the mean

On March 26, 1776, South Carolina adopted its first state constitution, shown here. John Rutledge was elected as its first state president. The signing of the state constitution was a milestone in the establishment of South Carolina. Not only did it establish South Carolina as a state, it marked the point when the state became free from British rule. With this break from the long arm of Britain, South Carolina took one step toward becoming a mature state and part of an emerging nation. **See page 56 for a transcription.**

and unless they all chose independence, the country would be divided.

In a debate held the day before the official vote, not all the delegates favored independence. New York decided not to vote, Delaware could not decide, and Pennsylvania and South Carolina were opposed to declaring independence from Great Britain.

South Carolina was just not certain that America was ready for independence. South Carolina also feared that if it became part of a new country, the northern states would try to end the slavery on which the state was heavily dependent. The next day, July 2, 1776, the official vote was taken. When all the votes were counted, all the states had voted for independence.

On July 4, 1776, Congress approved the Declaration of Independence, which had been written mainly by Virginia's Thomas Jefferson to explain why the thirteen colonies wanted to become the United States of America. Ever since then, Americans have celebrated July fourth as the birthday of their country.

When the declaration was read aloud in Charles Towne, the people cheered and paraded through the capital. However, although the states' decision to be independent was on paper, it still had to be won with bullets and cannonballs.

In 1780, British ships sailed past Fort Moultrie and began bombarding Charles Towne. Although the Americans tried to defend the city, Charles Towne fell to the British shortly thereafter. The British quickly overtook most of South Carolina and continued north into North Carolina.

When Camden, South Carolina was seized by the British, the town became the main British headquarters in South Carolina. The commander of the American forces in the South, General

Horatio Gates, wanted to take Camden from the British. However, the British learned of his plan. Gates and his 3,000 men were met by British general Charles Cornwallis and his 2,000 men as they approached the town on August 16, 1780.

The battle was a British victory. One thousand Americans were killed, and Gates and many of his men fled from the battlefield in terror. After Camden, the British felt they were invincible. However, they would soon find out that they were wrong.

On October 7, 1780, about 900 frontiersmen from North and South Carolina, Virginia, Tennessee, and Georgia attacked nearly 1,100 Loyalists under the command of British major Patrick Ferguson at Kings Mountain, in the northern part of South Carolina.

A tremendous battle was fought in which Major Ferguson and one-fifth of his men were killed. Another important victory for America was fought in South Carolina in a place called Cowpens, so named because cattle were penned there. General Daniel Morgan and his 1,000 men faced a slightly larger English force, led by Colonel Banastre Tarleton, there on January 17, 1781. Nearly all Tarleton's men were killed, wounded, or captured.

The colonial victories at Kings Mountain and Cowpens, as well as other places in the Carolinas, helped drive the British from South Carolina. In 1783, Great Britain signed the Treaty of Paris, which officially ended the Revolutionary War and recognized the thirteen states as a new nation—the United States of America.

The Eighth State

The new nation wrote a framework of government called the United States Constitution. Each state was to join the

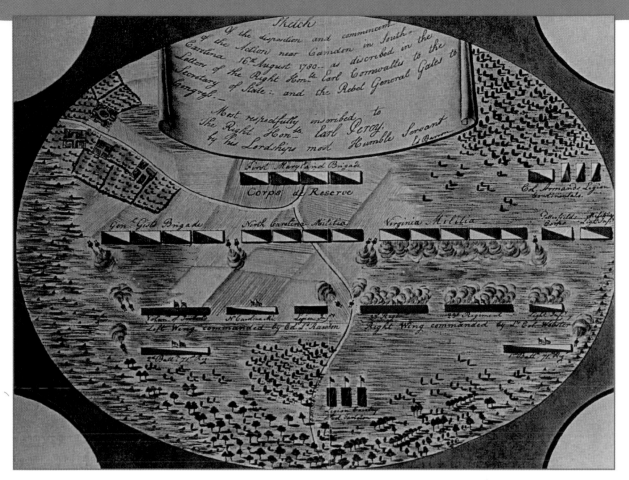

Shown here is a drawing of the Battle of Camden created for Lord Percy by Ed Barron. Camden was the headquarters of the British in America. When the American forces under General Horatio Gates tried to seize Camden from the British, the British fought back and won. General Charles Cornwallis's 2,000 men overcame the 3,000 American troops on August 16, 1780. One thousand Americans were killed in the battle. Though the British won this particular battle, they wouldn't win the war, as they soon found out.

country under the new constitution as it approved, or ratified, the paper.

In May 1788, South Carolina approved the United States Constitution and became the eighth state in the new nation.

John Rutledge became the state's first "governor." The city of Charles Towne was renamed Charleston, and, in 1790, the state capital was moved from there to Columbia, where it has remained ever since.

In the early 1800s, cotton became a very important crop in South Carolina. Many slaves were needed, however, to harvest the cotton. Many people from the northern states were against slavery. Therefore, when Abraham Lincoln, a Northerner, was elected president in 1860, many South Carolinians feared he would abolish slavery.

South Carolina became the first state to secede, or withdraw, from the union of thirteen states on December 20, 1860. Ten other states soon joined South Carolina, and they formed the Confederate States of America.

In April 1861, Confederate forces fired upon Fort Sumter, a Union-held fort in Charleston Harbor. These were the first shots of the Civil War, which lasted from 1861 to 1865.

South Carolina's economy suffered greatly during the war. Union ships blocked Charleston Harbor, making trade impossible. Union troops also burned the city of Columbia, along with many farms and plantations throughout the state.

After the Union won the Civil War in 1865, the South underwent Reconstruction. The Thirteenth Amendment to the U.S. Constitution freed the slaves, and the Fourteenth Amendment gave them the right to vote. On June 25, 1868, South Carolina was readmitted to the Union, but Union troops did not withdraw from the state until 1877.

South Carolinians have only begun in the last few decades to reclaim the kind of prosperity they knew before Reconstruction. The battle for civil rights was long fought in South Carolina.

John Rutledge, above, was chosen South Carolina's first state president on May 26, 1776 and later state governor in May 1788. Along with Rutledge's appointment as governor, South Carolina approved the United States Constitution and became the eighth state in the nation. These events marked a new chapter in South Carolina's history. The state capital was moved and its economy grew with the increased profitability of cotton. The state would also see the near collapse of the nation with the Civil War. Rutledge led the state into this new era.

Battles were fought over issues such as the right to vote and school desegregation, and, by the 1970s, most segregation had ended in South Carolina.

Today, the residents of South Carolina are mainly employed by the manufacturing and tourism businesses. Visitors to the state can enjoy magnificent plantation museums and gardens, broad beaches and golf courses, and Revolutionary and Civil War monuments, all evidence of South Carolina's wealth in both tradition and pride.

TIMELINE

1521 —— Francisco Gordillo explores the Carolina coast.

1526 —— The first settlement in South Carolina is attempted by Spaniard Lucas Vásquez de Ayllón.

1562 —— French Huguenots, led by Jean Ribault, settle on Parris Island.

1566 —— Spanish settle on Parris Island and remain there until 1587.

1629 —— King Charles I claims present-day North and South Carolina for England and names them Carolana.

1663 —— King Charles II gives Carolina to eight lords proprietors.

1670 —— The first permanent white settlement in South Carolina is established by the English at Albemarle Point.

1680 —— The Albemarle Point colony is moved to the site of present-day Charleston.

1689 —— The Huguenots settle at Jamestown in the Santee Swamp.

1712 —— Carolina is separated into North and South Carolina.

1715 —— The Yemassee War begins.

1739 —— The Stono Rebellion occurs.

1765 —— The Stamp Act is put into effect, and the Sons of Liberty of South Carolina organize.

1776 —— Colonists win the battle at Fort Moultrie on Sullivans Island on June 28.

1776 —— South Carolina signs the Declaration of Independence.

1780 —— Charles Towne is captured by the British on May 12.

1788 —— South Carolina becomes the eighth state of the Union on May 23.

1790 —— The state capital moves from Charles Towne to Columbia.

1860 —— South Carolina becomes the first state to secede from the Union.

1868 —— South Carolina is readmitted to the Union.

PRIMARY SOURCE TRANSCRIPTIONS

Page 16: Excerpt of the *Fundamental Constitutions of Carolina*

Transcription
THE Fundamental Constitutions of CAROLINA.
OUR SOVERAIGN LORD THE KING having out of His Royal Grace and Bounty, granted unto us the Province of Carolina, with all the Royalties, Proprieties, Jurisdictions, and Priviledges of a County Palatine [property of a high officer], as large and ample as the County Palatine of Durham, with other great Priviledges, for the better settlement of the Government of the said Place, and establishing the Interest of the Lords Proprietors with Equality, and without Confusion, and that with government of this Province may be made most agreeable [pleasing] to the Monarchy under which we live, and of which this Province is a part; and that we may avoid erecting [building] a numerous Democracy, we the Lords and Proprietors of the Province aforesaid [mentioned], have agreed to this following Form of Government, to be perpetually [forever] established among us, unto which we do oblige our selves, our Heirs and Successors, in the most binding ways that can be devised.

Page 22: Excerpt of *A Short Description of the Province of South-Carolina* by George Milligen-Johnston

Transcription
CHAP. V.
Of the Diseases most frequent in Charles-town and its Neighbourhood.
SECTION I.
THE Diseases, that may be termed Epidemics, are either acute or chronic: The acute Diseases may be subdivided into those of the warm and those of the cold Seasons.

The first are Intermittents [seasonal diseases] of all Kinds, Fluxes, and Cholera Morbus: The Winter Diseases are Pleurisies [lung diseases], Peripneumonies [pneumonia], and Catarrhal [sinus] Fevers.

The Chronic Diseases are Obstructions of the Abdominal Viscera [organs], Haemorrhoids, Ruptures, Worm-fevers, and what is called Lame Distemper.

Page 25: Excerpt of the *South-Carolina Gazette*, from Saturday, February 21 to Saturday, February 28, 1735–1736

Transcription
2 Old Man. Sir I understand you deal in Curiosities [souvenirs]. Have you any Thing in your Shop at present, that's pretty and curious?
Mast. Yes, Sir, I have a great many things. But the most ancient Curiosity I have got, is a small Brass Plate on which is engrav'd [written] the Speech which Adam made to his Wife, on their first Meeting, together with her answer. The Characters [words], thro' Age are grown unintelligible [unreadable]: But for that 'tis the more to be valued. What is remarkable in this ancient Piece is, that Eve's Speech is about three times as long as her Husband's. I have a Ram's Horn, one of those which help'd to blow down the Wall of Jericho. A Lock of Sampson's Hair, tied up in a Shred of Joseph's Garment. With several other Jewish Antiquities [antiques], which I purchas'd of that Profile at a great Price. Then I have the Tune which Orpheus play'd to the Devil, when he charmed back his Wife.
Gent. That was thought to be a silly Tune, I believe, for no body has ever car'd [cared] to learn it since.

Page 34: Excerpt of the *Journal of the Commons House of Assembly*

Transcription
Mr. Mazyck from the Comm'ee [Committee] appointed to consider of proper means to relieve the People about Stono from the dangers arising from domestic Enemys: who were also appointed to a Comm'ee to consider-of, and to report to this House, the most

effectual [effective] means for prevention of such dangers throughout the Province [colony], made a Report which he first read in his place, and then delivered it in at the Table. And the same was again afterwards read to the House, and is in the Words following . . .

The Comm'ee appointed to consider the proper means to relieve the People about Stono from the dangers arising from domestic Enemys; and to consider of the most effectual means from prevention of such dangers throughout the Province.

Page 37: Excerpt of the Muster Roll and Pay List of Colonel George Gabriel's Company, expedition to Fort Prince George

Transcription
Muster Roll and Pay List of Colonel George Gabriel Powell's Batallion Serving on the late Expedition against the Cherokees from the 18th day of October 1759 to the 15th day of January 1760. Inclusive (i.e.) Ninety Seven Days under the Command of his Excellency William Henry Lyttelton Esquire Governour and Captain General.

Page 39: Excerpt of The Stamp Act

Transcription
George III. Regis.
An Act for granting and applying certain Stamp duties, and other duties, in the British Colonies and Plantations in America, towards further defraying [paying for] the Expences of defending, protecting, and securing the same; and for amending [changing] such Parts of the several Acts of Parliament relating to the Trade and Revenues of the said colonies and Plantations, as direct the Manner of determining and recovering the Penalties and Forfeitures therein mentioned.

Page 44: Excerpt of the South Carolina Constitution

Transcription

In a Congress begun and held at Charles-Town on Wednesday the first Day of November, One thousand, seven hundred and seventy five and continued by divers adjourning to Tuesday the twenty sixth day of March, One thousand seven hundred and seventy six:

A Constitution on Form of Government agrees to and Resolved upon by the Representatives of South-Carolina.

Whereas the British Parliament claiming of late years a Right, to bind the North American Colonies by law in all cases whatsoever, have Enacted statutes for raising a Revenue in those colonies and disposing of such Revenue as they thought proper without the consent and against the will of the colonists. And whereas it appearing to them that (they not being represented in Parliament) such claim was altogether unconstitutional, and if admitted would at once, reduce them, from the rank of Freemen to a state of the most abject [worst] slavery, the said colonies must severally remonstrated [protested] against the passing, and petitioned for the repeal of those acts, but in vain.

GLOSSARY

colony A group of people who settle in a foreign land but are still governed by the ruler of their native land.

Confederates The political group that seceded from the Union during the Civil War.

Continental Congress The government that the colonists formed in 1774 in opposition to Britain.

lords proprietors Men who were given a colony for which they had the power to make the laws and who could rent or sell the land as they wished.

militia An army made up of civilians, or ordinary citizens.

Parliament The British governing body.

petition A formal, written document or a collection of signatures requesting a right or benefit from an authority.

Pilgrims Protestants from England who settled in present-day Massachusetts.

plantation A large plot of land that produces crops for sale.

Reconstruction The time between 1865 and 1877 when states that had seceded from the Union were controlled by the federal government.

reservation Land that was set aside by the United States federal government for the Native Americans to live on.

secession The act of formally withdrawing from a group.

segregation The separation of people by race or religion.

treaty A peace agreement between two or more groups.

Union The states that were loyal to the United States during the Civil War.

FOR MORE INFORMATION

Charleston Museum
360 Meeting Street
Charleston, SC 29403
(843) 722-2996
Web site: http://www.charlestonmuseum.org

Children's Museum of South Carolina
2501 North Kings Highway
Myrtle Beach, SC 29578
(843) 946-9469
Web site: http://www.cmsckids.org

South Carolina Department of Archives and History
8301 Parklane Road
Columbia, SC 29223
(803) 896-6100
Web site: http://www.state.sc.us/scdah

South Carolina Historical Society
100 Meeting Street
Charleston, SC 29401
(843) 723-3225
Web site: http://www.schistory.org

Web Sites

Due to the changing nature of Internet links, the Rosen Publishing Group, Inc., has developed an online list of Web sites related to the subject of this book. This site is updated regularly. Please use this link to access the list:

http://www.rosenlinks.com/pstc/soca

FOR FURTHER READING

Alderman, Clifford Lindsey. *The Story of the Thirteen Colonies*. New York, NY: Random House, 1966.

Stein, Conrad R. *South Carolina*. Danbury, CT: Children's Press, 1999.

Taylor, Alan. *American Colonies*. New York, NY: Viking Penguin, 2001.

Whitehurst, Susan. *The Colony of South Carolina.* (The Library of the Thirteen Colonies and the Lost Colony). New York, NY: PowerKids Press, 2000.

Wilcox, Charlotte. *South Carolina*. Mankato, MN: Capstone Press, 1997.

BIBLIOGRAPHY

Burney, Eugenia. *Colonial South Carolina*. Nashville, TN: Thomas Nelson, Inc., 1970.

Edgar, Walter. *South Carolina: A History*. Columbia, SC: University of South Carolina Press, 1998.

Fradin, Dennis Brindell. *The South Carolina Colony*. Danbury, CT: Children's Press, 1992.

Kent, Deborah. *America the Beautiful: South Carolina*. Danbury, CT: Children's Press, 1989.

Weir, Robert M. *Colonial South Carolina: A History*. New York, NY: KTO Press, 1983.

PRIMARY SOURCE IMAGE LIST

Title Page: Painting titled A *View of Charlestown the Capital of South Carolina in North America*. 1767. Housed in the Mariners' Museum in Newport News, Virginia.

Page 5: Painting titled *Floridae Americae* by Theodore de Bry. It is housed in the New York Public Library in New York.

Page 8: Colored woodcut titled *The Holy Communion of the Protestants and Ride to Hell of the Catholics*. Located in Staatliche Museen zu Berlin in Berlin, Germany.

Page 10: Painting titled *Spanish Expeditions Employed Indians to Carry Equipment* by Theodore de Bry. Housed in the New York Public Library in New York.

Page 12: Oil painting of Gaspard de Coligny, Lord of Chatillon, Admiral of France. Located in the Bibliothèque de l'Histoire du Protestantisme in Paris, France.

Page 13: Painting by Theodore de Bry, from *Americae* part II, 1591. Housed in Staatliche Museen zu Berlin in Berlin, Germany.

Page 16 (top): The Fundamental Constitutions of Carolina by John Locke, 1669. Housed in the Rare Book and Special Collections division of the Library of Congress in Washington, D.C.

Page 16 (bottom): Oil on canvas painting of King Charles II by Sir Peter Lely. Housed in the Royal Hospital Chelsea in London, England.

Page 19: 1704 plan of Charles Towne by Edward Crisp. Housed in the South Carolina Department of Archives and History in Columbia, South Carolina.

Page 22: *A Short Description of the Province of South-Carolina* by George Milligen-Johnston. 1763. Housed in the New York Public Library in New York.

Page 24: Drawing of Kahal Kadosh Beth Elohim synagogue, circa 1812, by John Rubens Smith. Housed in the Library of Congress in Washington, D.C.

Page 25: The *South-Carolina Gazette*, February 21–February 28, 1735–1736. Housed in the New York Public Library in New York.

Page 26: Illustration on map entitled "South Carolina and a Part of Georgia," by William de Brahm. Housed in the South Caroliniana Library at the University of South Carolina in Columbia, South Carolina.

Page 28: Slave advertisement in the *South-Carolina Gazette*, January 3–January 10, 1735–1736. Housed in the New York Public Library in New York.

Page 31: Engraving of Blackbeard the pirate, 1724. From *A General History of the Robberies and Murders of the Most Notorious Pyrates* by Daniel Defoe.

Page 33: *Portrait of George I* by Hermann Goldschmidt. Housed in the Musée du Château de Versailles in Versailles, France.

Page 34: *Journal of the Commons House of Assembly*, 1739. Housed in the South Carolina Department of Archives and History in Columbia, South Carolina.

Page 37: Muster roll and pay list for Colonel George Gabriel's company, expedition to Fort Prince George, 1759. Housed in the South Carolina Department of Archives and History in Columbia, South Carolina.

Page 39 (top): The Stamp Act, 1765. Printed by Mark Baskett. Housed in the Library of Congress in Washington, D.C.

Page 39 (bottom): Proof Sheet of 1d Stamp Duties for Newspapers, 1765. Housed in the British Library in London, England.

Page 41: Portraits of Edward Rutledge and Christopher Gadsden. Housed in the University of South Carolina Library in Columbia, South Carolina.

Page 44: Constitution of South Carolina, 1776. Housed in the South Carolina Department of Archives and History in Columbia, South Carolina.

Page 47: Battle of Camden map drawn for Lord Percy by Ed Barron. Housed at the Public Archives of Nova Scotia in Halifax, Canada.

Page 49: Portrait of John Rutledge by John Trumbull, circa 1791. Housed in the National Portrait Gallery, Smithsonian Institution in Washington, D.C.

INDEX

About the Author

Heather Elizabeth Hasan is a writer from Greencastle, Pennsylvania, where she lives with her husband, Omar, and their son, Samuel. Much of what she knows about South Carolina she learned from childhood trips she took to this great state. She has written numerous books for the Rosen Publishing Group, including *American Women of the Gulf War*.

Photo Credits

Editor: Nicholas Croce; **Photo Researcher:** Amy Feinberg